THE END OF AN ERA

OTHER WORKS BY THE AUTHOR

POWER TO THE PEOPLE
A New Model for Collective Ownership to Increase the Democratic and Sustainable Nature of Electrical Utilities

THE LOCAL ELECTRIC LIGHT UTILITY
A Survey of Collectively-Owned Local Electrical Utilities in America and Opportunities for Australia

AN SEANN TAIGH
The History and Vernacular Architecture of the Old Glebe House at Piper's Cove
(CO-AUTHORED WITH ROCHELLE MACQUEEN)

THE END OF AN ERA

*A Portrait of the
Former Nova Scotian
Town of Canso*

M. G. MADER

DOWNINGFIELD PRESS PROPRIETARY LIMITED
NAARM / MELBOURNE · UNAMA'KI / CAPE BRETON

www.downingfield.com · mail@downingfield.com

PO Box 92
FAWKNER VICTORIA 3060
Australia

Tenth Anniversary Edition (paperback)
Second Printing February 2022

First published as *The End of an Era: A Portrait of the Town of Canso as it Prepares to Dissolve* in 2012 (paperback) by the Canso Booklet Committee of the Caper Times Division of Book Publishing. Reprinted in 2013 (paperback) by M. G. Mader Publishing Services. A facsimile version of the 2012 first edition was published by Downingfield Press in 2019 (e-book).

This Tenth Anniversary Edition published by Downingfield Press, January 2022. Text and illustrations copyright © M. G. Mader 2012, 2022, unless otherwise stated. The photograph on page 12 of the Western Union Telegraph Company office in Canso is used with permission of the Nova Scotia Archives.

The moral right of the author has been asserted.

All Rights Reserved.

Without limiting the rights under copyright reserved above, in accordance with the Copyright Act 1968 (Commonwealth of Australia) no part of this publication may be reproduced, stored in or introduced into a retrieval system, or transmitted, in any form or by any means (electronic, mechanical, xerographic, recording, or otherwise), without the prior written permission of the copyright owner and the publisher of this book.

Although the publisher and the author have made every effort to ensure that the information in this book was correct at press time and while this publication is designed to provide accurate information in regard to the subject matter covered, the publisher and the author assume no responsibility for errors, inaccuracies, omissions, or any other inconsistencies herein and hereby disclaim any liability to any party for any loss, damage, or disruption caused by errors or omissions, whether such errors or omissions result from negligence, accident, or any other cause.

ISBN 978-0-9959217-3-3 (paperback)

Cover photograph copyright © M. G. Mader 2012, 2022.

A joint Australian-Canadian publication.

 A catalogue record for this work is available from the National Library of Australia

The seal of the former Town of Canso. The seal consists of a central scene showing a fisherman fishing from a wooden dory, with a schooner sailing in the background, behind which is an island with a lighhouse. The town flag consists of a white field with the town seal centred in the middle.

The welcome sign at the Canso town limits as it appeared in June 2012 prior to dissolution. This sign was replaced by a Municipality of the District of Guysborough branded sign after Canso dissolved and amalgamated into the District of Guysborough.

YOUR OWN LITTLE TOWN

There are fancier towns than your own little town,
There are towns that are bigger than this;
And people who live in the tinier towns,
Don't know what excitement they miss;
There are things you can see in a wealthier town,
That you can't in a town that is small;
And yet, up and down, there is no other town,
Like your own little town after all.

AUTHOR UNKNOWN

The Hazel Hill Commercial Cable Station, shown above as it appeared in 2012, was built in 1884 and operated until 1962 when it was abandoned. This was the telegraph station that first received news of the Titanic disaster in 1912, a century before the town's dissolution. Whilst the building was not within the town limits, it is an important landmark in the area and no book about Canso would be complete without it.

A committee was struck to save the building and the group managed to purchase the property in 2006. The group sought to restore the building and develop it into a community asset. The group raised the funds required to restore the building but unfortunately an anchor tenant could not be found which meant the future maintenance costs could not be met. The committee thus surrendered the property to the ownership of the Municipality of the District of Guysborough.

The municipality had an engineer assess the building and it was found to be in a state of disrepair, with the internal floors having collapsed and the roof in a precarious state. Sadly, the municipality was forced to condemn the building and it was demolished in September 2017. The granite foundation was saved and the committee intends to erect interpretive panels to tell the history of the building.

INTRODUCTION

Canso, Nova Scotia was founded in A.D. 1604 as a British outpost during the period of European settlement when the French and English fought for control of what is now eastern Canada. The settlement was incorporated as a town in 1901, nearly three centuries after its founding, when it separated from the Municipality of the District of Guysborough.

Situated at the north-easterly most tip of mainland Nova Scotia, the town has played a major role in both the Atlantic fisheries and in transatlantic communication between the old and new worlds. In its heyday, the town was home to two major telegraph cable stations and was the site where the first messages telling of the Titanic disaster were received in mainland North America.

The town is also home to the Canso Islands National Historic Site of Canada which played a significant role in the battle for Louisbourg between the British and French during the 17th century.

In recent years, the prominence of the town has diminished with the collapse of the Atlantic cod fishery and the impacts of deindustrialisation being experienced across Nova Scotia and the Maritimes as a whole.

The idea behind this book was to show the Town of Canso as it was in its final days as an independent community. It is a portrait of the town whilst the local electric light utility was still in operation, Canso Academy remained open, and the town still had self-government (and duplicate sets of electricity poles and wires in some streets as the local utility and Nova Scotia Power competed to serve the town's largest customer: the fish processing plant). This is not a history of the Town of Canso but rather a portrait of the town – a snapshot of a certain time and place – at the close of one era and the beginning of another. Many of the public buildings in the town have since been demolished but are forever preserved in this publication.

This updated second edition includes new commentary sourced from recorded interviews with the town's last mayor, Mr Frank Fraser, which were not printed in the first edition. At the time this book was originally published, there was some sensitivity surrounding the dissolution of the town, as well as significant pressure around the deadline to finalise the book. The original edition was put together in less than a fortnight in order for the book to be handed out to the attendees of the town closing ceremony on 10 June 2012. Now, eight years later, this updated second edition seeks to fill the gaps of the original publication.

When this book was originally published, Canso was the first town since the millennium to surrender its charter and dissolve its town government. Over the past eight years, five more towns have also relinquished their local government status.

In 2015, Nova Scotia lost three towns when Bridgetown dissolved and became a part of the Municipality of the County of Annapolis, Springhill was absorbed into the Municipality of the County of Cumberland, and Hantsport became an unincorporated community within the Municipality of the District of West Hants. In 2016, the Town of Parrsboro dissolved and became a part of the Municipality of the County of Cumberland. The Village of Harve Boucher dissolved in 2018. Indeed, this introduction had to be revised in the midst of production due to the dissolution of the Town of Windsor on 1 April 2020, when it joined the Municipality of the District of West Hants to form the new West Hants Regional Municipality and further revisions were required just weeks prior to publication in late 2021 when the Village of Baddeck announced its intention to hold a vote to allow ratepayers to determine whether or not to dissolve the Village Commission.

The dissolution of a town was a rare event when this book was originally written but such events now seem relatively commonplace and the future of the province's remaining towns has certainly been called into question. Nova Scotia lost all of its incorporated cities in the 1990s when municipalities in Cape Breton and Halifax counties were amalgamated into new 'regional' municipalities. It would seem that the province's towns will face difficulty in surviving the present century if the current rate of town dissolutions continue. Whether the current circumstances facing the towns of Nova Scotia are indicative of the long-term decline of the province or poor policy on behalf of the provincial and federal governments is for history to judge.

Regardless of the cause, every town that dissolves further removes democracy from the hands of Nova Scotians who move from being governed by local town councillors – neighbours – to regional councillors, who are often neither locals nor neighbours.

In the 2021 Nova Scotia provincial election, it was noted in the press that several provincial constituencies in the Halifax Regional Municipality were smaller than the counterpart municipal districts. It is indicative of the poor state of Nova Scotia local governance that the ratio of constituents to provincial MLAs is smaller than the ratio of constituents to municipal councillors in some municipalities. The real life consequences of this discrepancy is that councillors in amalgamated regional municipalities are often not known to the citizens they represent and, as a result, it is often impossible for such councillors to be fully aware of the issues faced by the citizens they represent due to the sheer number of constituents and the unreasonably large geographic area each councillor is responsible for representing.

Photo used with permission of Nova Scotia Archives (Notman Studio Nova Scotia Archives 1983-310 number 63482).

The Western Union Telegraph Company building in Canso in the early 20th century (likely before 1920). This building eventually became the Canso Town Hall after Western Union closed their Canso office and the building was acquired by the Town of Canso. Canso served as the landing point for the main telegraph lines connecting Europe with North America.

The Town Office in 2012. The former town office was located at 11 Telegraph Street and was housed in the building which once served as the Western Union telegraph station until it closed in the 1950s. The building was purchased by the Town of Canso in 1956, renovated, and became the first permanent town office. It served as the offices of the Town of Canso until dissolution in 2012. The building was designated as a 'Town of Canso Heritage Property'.

The last Mayor of the Town of Canso, His Worship Frank Fraser, at his desk in the town office in June 2012. The mayor of a small town such as Canso does much of his work himself and takes a very hands-on approach to government. Mr Fraser was kind enough to provide the author with a tour of the town during the preparation of this publication in 2012.

The town Council chamber within the town office as it appeared in June 2012 just prior to dissolution. During a town Council meeting, the mayor was seated at the front as chairman, directly below a portrait of Her Majesty the Queen and between the provincial and national flags. A special gavel used by the mayor when chairing the meetings and a copy of the Bible were kept at the mayor's desk in the chamber for use when swearing in witnesses presenting to the town Council.

His worship Frank Fraser seated at his desk in the town council chamber at the town office in June 2012.

The Town of Canso Heritage Property plaque mounted on the outside of the Canso Town Office building in June 2012. Originally intended to be the beginning of a municipal heritage property programme, this plaque was the only Town of Canso Heritage Property registered by the Town of Canso according to the last mayor of Canso, Frank Fraser.

The Canso Islands National Historic Site of Canada once featured a fortress, Fort William Augustus. The island was the site of the original settlement known as Canso and the fortress and island played a major role in the battles for Louisbourg during the 18th century. The islands were once the area of choice for settlement due to the risk of wild animals and conflict with the indigenous population on the mainland, but over time the entire population eventually resettled on the mainland at the present location of Canso.

Today, the islands can be visited as part of the Canso Islands National Historic Site of Canada. The exhibits demonstrate what life was like for island residents in 1743.

The Canso Islands National Historic's Site of Canada was declared in 1925 in recognition of the islands' historical role in the development of British North America. Grassy Island was also individually designated as the Grassy Island National Historic Site of Canada in 1962. The interpretive centre is located on the mainland in Canso.

Canso remained an unincorporated settlement from its founding in the 17th-century until 1901, when the community was incorporated as a town with its own municipal government. The Municipality of the District of Guysborough was established in 1879 when county governments were incorporated across Nova Scotia. Canso was part of the District Municipality from 1879 until 1901 and once again became part of the District Municipality since the dissolution of the town in 2012.

The town of Canso was unique in being one of the few municipalities within Nova Scotia to operate a municipal electric light utility. Canso, being located in a relatively remote part of mainland Nova Scotia, established an electric light utility, owned by the citizens of Canso through the town, in 1914 with the opening of a small coal-fired generating station. The town commissioned the construction of a power generating plant so that the streets of the town could be lit with electric light. The estimated construction cost of the plant was $15,000 (approximately $340,000 as of 2020) but the final bill came to $17,000 (approximately

View of the central part of the town as seen from the cemetery of Star of the Sea Roman Catholic church. Canso Academy (now demolished) can be seen in the centre of the photograph.

The Canso Islands National Historic Site of Canada interpretive centre and wharf, from which the summer ferry service operates to transport visitors to the Canso Islands National Historic Site of Canada and the Grassy Island National Historic Site of Canada, both of which can be seen in the background.

A view of Grassy Island, with Eastern Memorial Hospital in the foreground.

The Town of Canso Electric Light Utility's boom truck. This was the only boom truck owned by the Town at the time of dissolution.

$385,000 as of 2020) by the time the project was completed due to cost overruns caused by unforeseen issues.

The town also operated a hydroelectric utility for a period of time during the 20th century, but later began purchasing electricity wholesale from the Nova Scotia Power Commission and, later, the Nova Scotia Power Corporation. At the time of dissolution, the town sourced its electricity exclusively from Nova Scotia Power which it then onsold to the citizens of the town at a discount which equated to roughly 3 cents below the retail prices paid by other Nova Scotians within the jurisdiction of the privatised Nova Scotia Power.

In 2012, in the lead up to the dissolution of the town of Canso, Canadian British Consultants Limited (CBCL) were undertaking investigations into the future viability of the town's electric light utility. CBCL attempted to find interested parties to purchase the utility, but the only interested party was Nova Scotia Power. The last mayor of Canso, Frank Fraser, preferred to see the utility continue independent of the town as a cooperative, but noted that lack of human and financial resources meant the possibility of this happening was highly unlikely. Moreover, the District Municipality, which took over governance of Canso on 1 July 2012, was not interested in continuing to operate the utility. Mr Fraser noted the amalgamation would force the loss of the utility and he expected that the utility would be sold within a year of dissolution.

During the time that Canso operated its own electric light utility, it had linesmen working exclusively within the town who were able to respond within minutes to a power outage or issue and, as a result, the town was noted for its lack of sustained power outages — events which are all too common in other parts of the province without their own local utility.

The utility continued to operate under the auspices of the District Municipality whilst the regulatory bureaucracy was navigated to gain approval to sell the utility. On 22 October 2019, the provincial regulator – the Nova Scotia Utility and Review Board – approved the sale of the assets of the Canso Electric Light Utility by the Municipality of the District of

Guysborough to Nova Scotia Power Incorporated for one dollar, to transfer the former town of Canso into the jurisdiction of Nova Scotia Power, and expand the approved Nova Scotia Power retail rates to cover Canso. The transfer took effect on 1 January 2020, nearly 8 years after the dissolution of the town.

Whilst the conclusion of Canso's independent electric light utility was regrettable as it further consolidates the provincial electricity market into a single private monopoly, the assets of the utility making up the town's electricity grid were in need of major repairs and modernisation. The cost of these works will be significant and the District municipality, which did not operate a utility prior to absorbing Canso, noted it did not have the resources to undertake these works. As part of the Utility and Review Board order approving the transfer of the utility to Nova Scotia Power, a capital works order was approved to take effect at the time of the transfer that would see the immediate commencement of upgrading the town's electricity network and infrastructure.

His Worship H. A. Rice, mayor of the town of Canso, switched on the electric light in Canso on 15 October 1914. This lit the streets of Canso for the first time. The utility continued to operate for over a century and outlived the town of Canso itself until it ended on the first day of 2020. Thus, after 106 years, the Canso Electric Light Utility was unceremoniously wound up and another era came to a close.

Canso Academy was the town's high school. It closed the same year that the town dissolved. The secondary school was merged with the existing primary school, Fanning Education Centre, which lies just outside the town limits in Hazel Hill, to form a comprehensive school educating all grades from primary through 12.

The previous Academy, a wooden structure, burnt in the 1940s and the building shown on page 29 was reconstructed in 1944. The town of Canso originally operated the education system before the town system was amalgamated into the county school board system serving all of Guysborough County. In the late 1990s, the county boards across the province

Detail of the Town of Canso decal on the passenger door of the Town of Canso Electric Light Utility's single boom truck, which serviced the town's electricity grid infrastructure.

were further consolidated into regional school boards, with the town falling under the Strait Regional School Board. The regional school board system operated until 2018 when a province-wide reform dissolved all elected school boards and replaced them with branches of the Department of Education staffed by career civil servants.

The result of the numerous mergers of school systems has been to erode the accountability of the public school system to the electors, whose children the system educates. At one time, school-related issues could be raised with the members of the town council – community members who were local and accessible. Under the county school board system the town elected a single representative – at one time the representative was Mr Frank Fraser, who was also the last mayor of the town – to ensure the interests of the townspeople were being upheld. The regional school board system saw the town share a single elected representative with half of the county, which reduced the accessibility of the representative but ensured the townspeople could still have their say at the ballot box when the representative was elected.

The 2018 reforms have resulted in the absolute removal and abolishment of democracy from the Nova Scotia public school system. Citizens no longer have a say at the ballot box in regard to who administers the education system that is funded by Nova Scotians and exists to educate the future generations of the province. Civil servants now make the decisions, taking direction from the Minister for Education.

This mural located in the grounds of the town office depicting historic scenes from Canso' past was painted by the artist Nick Avery in 1999.

The Canso branch of the Bank of Montreal, which has had a presence in Canso since 1894. The branch pictured above opened in 1964 at 28 Main Street. The Bank of Montreal sponsored the original 2012 edition of this publication and helped make possible this extensive collection of photographs of Canso in its final days as an incorporated town contained in this book.

Canso Academy with the historic cairn in foreground as it appeared in June 2012. Canso Academy closed shortly after this photo was taken and has since been demolished. The cairn remains in place.

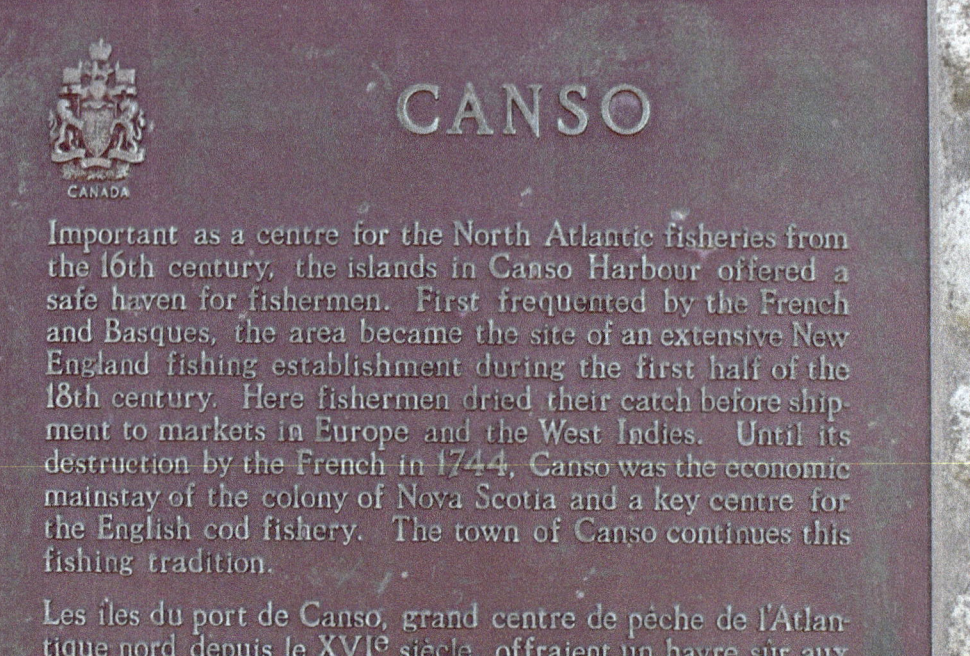

The plaque shown above is affixed to an historic cairn which sits in the frontage of what was once Canso Academy.

The former Canso Town Library, located across the street from the site of the former Canso Academy, as it appeared in June 2012, which has now been replaced by a new building in another location within Canso.

The Canso Enterprise Centre, originally constructed as the Canso Post Office and Dominion Customs Office. The building is similar in design to numerous other post office buildings built in the same era across Canada.

Canso's modern post office as it appeared in 2012. The door to the right of the photo contained a federal fisheries office, which has since been converted into a café (as of 2016).

The Canso Enterprise Centre was originally known as the Canso Public Building when it opened in 1906 and housed the post office and customs office. The building was designed by David Ewart, Chief Architect of the Dominion Government's Department of Public Works, who designed many public buildings between 1889 and 1915 throughout Canada.

A modern post office was erected in the postwar period and also housed a fisheries office which, as of 2016, has been converted into a café.

The Canso public building has undergone changes over its century of existence. The clock in the tower was not installed until March 1909 and the building was originally lit by a gas lighting system that was installed in July 1909, only five years before electric light would come to the town with the founding of the Canso Electric Light Utility. In 1944, the building burnt to the ground in a fire with only the brick façade remaining, but was restored to its former glory through the hard work and dedication of the people of Canso. It is noted that Canso Academy also burnt in 1944 but it is unknown if the fires were connected.

The building was sold to a private owner when the new post office opened. In 1991, the town of Canso acquired the building and operated it as the Canso Enterprise Centre. Since 1991, the building has housed the offices of the local member of the provincial legislature and a call centre, amongst other things.

A SIGN OF THE TIMES

While the dissolution might be a sad situation for some people in Canso, it is a sign of the times. More and more responsibilities are being downloaded onto municipalities by both the provincial and, indirectly, federal governments to the point where many municipalities in Nova Scotia are having a great deal of trouble coping, and unfortunately Canso has been the first casualty. Nevertheless, Canso, as a place, will never lose its identity, it will always be Canso with the same long history of fishing and marine related activity.

HER WORSHIP MARNEY SIMMONS
MAYOR OF THE NEIGHBOURING TOWN OF MULGRAVE
AT THE TIME OF DISSOLUTION IN 2012

An historic view of Canso presented in a mural on the side of the Canso telephone exchange building. The mural was painted by the artist 'Peter' in 1996. Canso was connected to the Maritime Telephone and Telegraph Company's (MT&T) telephone network, now part of Bell Aliant, in 1908.

The Canso and Area Arena, left, was built in 1982 and the Town of Canso Community Pool, right, was built in 1989. These facilities, along with baseball diamonds, formed the Town of Canso Recreational Complex prior to the dissolution of the town in 2012.

Canso has long been home to an industrious people committed to improving their community. Alongside the work of the town in procuring affordable electric light for the town and developing a community enterprise centre, the townspeople established the Canso Medical Centre, pictured above, as a cooperative to serve the community. The facility includes a helipad to accommodate transfers from Canso's 15 bed Eastern Memorial Hospital to larger facilities in Halifax. The hospital also houses a 15 bed aged care facility to care for the town's aged.

The town contracted policing services to the RCMP. Prior to dissolution, it was agreed that the Mounties would maintain a presence in the town after dissolution.

The Nova Scotia Liquor Corporation's Canso shop, built 1988. The Government of Nova Scotia holds a monopoly on liquor sales and operates government-owned shops in communities throughout the province. Proceeds from the sale of liquor and, since its legalisation in 2018, cannabis go back to government to assist with the upkeep and operation of the province's hospitals, schools, and other essential government services.

The historic Canso Garage, built 1950, located at the corner of Main and School Streets. At the time this photograph was taken, the garage remained in operation as part of the Wilson's chain of petrol stations.

Looking down Telegraph Street towards the sea. The Town Office is to the right of the frame.

The Town of Canso war memorial, erected 1921.

Looking up Telegraph Street towards the town water supply tank. Sailor's Rest is to the right of the frame.

The Canso Public Works Building (now demolished), pictured above, was the headquarters of the Canso Electric Light Utility linesmen, as well as the town's public works unit. The only boom truck owned by the Town of Canso can be seen behind the building at the far left of the photo and some of the aged electricity infrastructure can be observed to the left of the building, including an aged streetlight. Noting that this photo was taken nearly a decade ago, one can imagine the state of the infrastructure 10 years on just prior to the transfer of the utility into the Nova Scotia Power network.

The Canso volunteer fire bridage, established in 1927 through a $7000 loan taken out by the Town of Canso to purchase fire fighting equipment.

The Canso Lions Club as it appeared in 2012. The Lions Club was an active civic organisation within Canso at the time this publication was originally written.

Star of the Sea Roman Catholic church, built circa 1876.

The Canso branch of the Royal Canadian Legion at the time of dissolution in 2012. The Legion is located across the street from the fire bridage.

The town's location on the north-eastern most tip of mainland Nova Scotia made an excellent landing site for transatlantic communication cables, indeed several cables still make landfall in Nova Scotia, albeit now near Halifax.

Whilst the days of the town being central to telecommunications have passed, in the past 10 years since dissolution the town has found itself at the centre of the space exploration industry.

In March 2017, after more than a year of extensive research and analysis of more than 12 locations across North America, Maritime Launch, a space exploration company, selected Canso as its future launch site for space vehicles. The town was chosen due to the favourable physics of launching a space vehicle from this part of the continent. The company currently maintains an office in Halifax, but will be relocating its offices to Canso once construction has finished. The facility is expected to be operational by late 2022 or early 2023. When the facility has been completed and is operating at full capacity, it is anticipated that more than 250 people could be employed at the facility during a launch campaign. There will also be other spin-off employment benefits for Canso and the surrounding area. The company has an initial 40-year lease of the land on which it will build the facility and anticipates that this lease will be extended when the first 40 years have passed.

As of late 2021, the company has announced it has at least one paying customer for its planned first launch in the middle of the decade. The company has indicated that the space exploration industry is expected to grow exponentially over the coming years, with Canso possibly at the centre of this global industry.

THE EMOTIONAL QUOTIENT

In 2012, Her Worship Marney Simmons, then-mayor of Mulgrave spoke of the dissolution of the Town of Canso and pointed to downloading by both the provincial and federal governments as a factor in the ability of small towns to cope. Since 2012, three other Nova Scotia towns have been dissolved, Bridgetown and Hantsport in 2014, Windsor in 2021 and the Village of Baddeck is now considering its future. Yet, the downloading continues unabated. For small towns to continue to be viable, we have to learn how to cope. This includes the ability to understand, use and manage our assets in positive ways, relieve stress, communicate effectively, empathize with others, overcome challenges and defuse conflict. Towns need to build stronger relationships, turn intention into action, and make informed decisions about what matters most to us (and if any of this sounds familiar, it's because these are some the elements of EQ, or what is known as the emotional quotient). In the end, you have to want to be a town to continue to be a town. But that doesn't mean that there aren't other viable options out there including amalgamations such as Queens Regional Municipality, NS and Grand Bay-Westfield, NB. As always, it is a matter of choice and will.

HER WORSHIP AMERY BOYER
MAYOR OF THE TOWN OF ANNAPOLIS ROYAL,
NOVA SCOTIA'S SMALLEST TOWN BY POPULATION

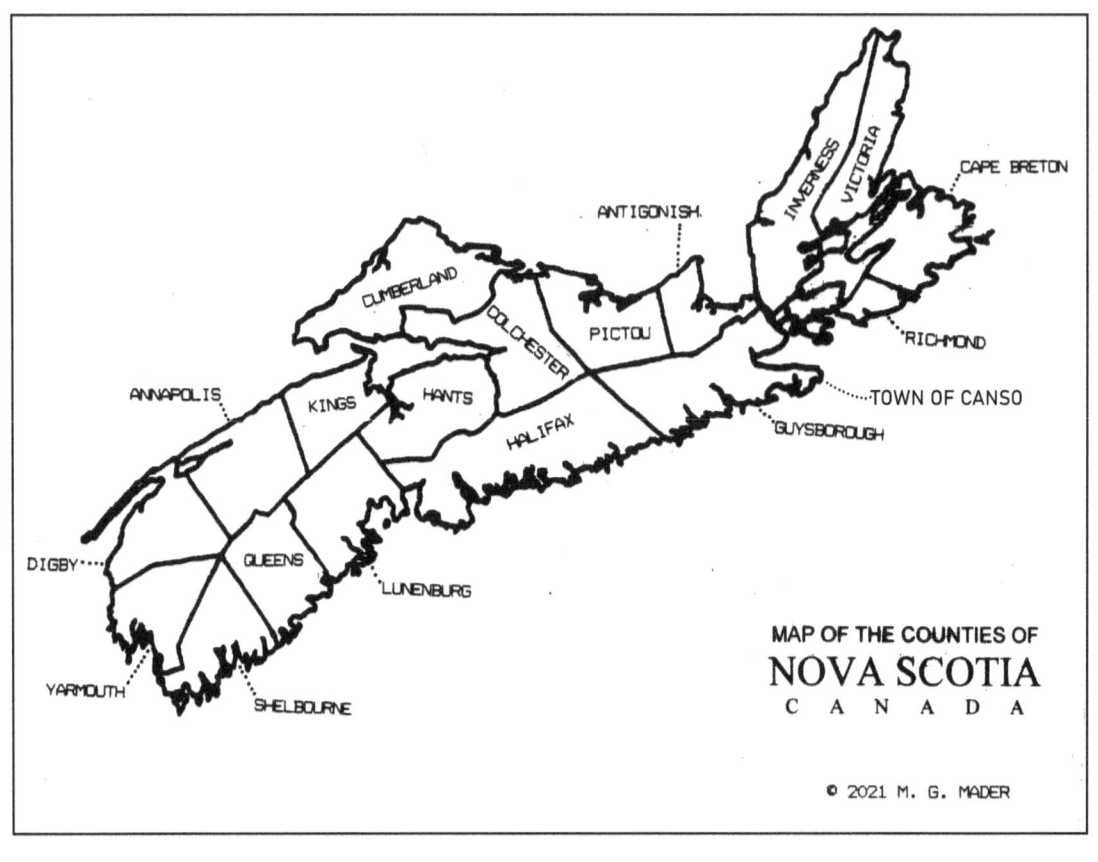

Map of the eighteen counties of Nova Scotia showing the location of Canso within the province.

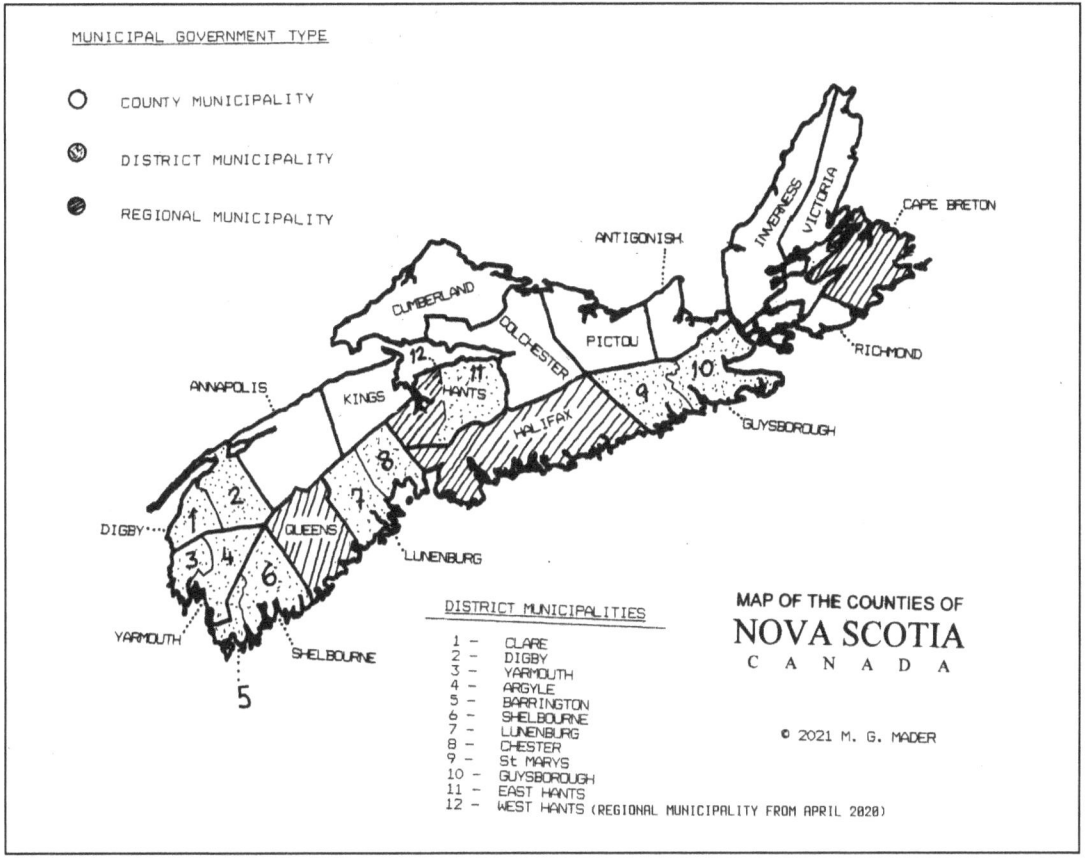

Map of Nova Scotia showing the type of municipal government in each county. Nova Scotia has four regional municipalities, with the municipality in West Hants being the newest. West Hants is also the only regional municipality that does not cover an entire county. Nine counties have a unified county municipal goverment, with some communities governed by incorporated towns and villages. Incorporated towns are not shown. Six counties are subdivided into district municipalities, which operate similarly to county municipalities and with some communities governed by incorporated towns and villages.

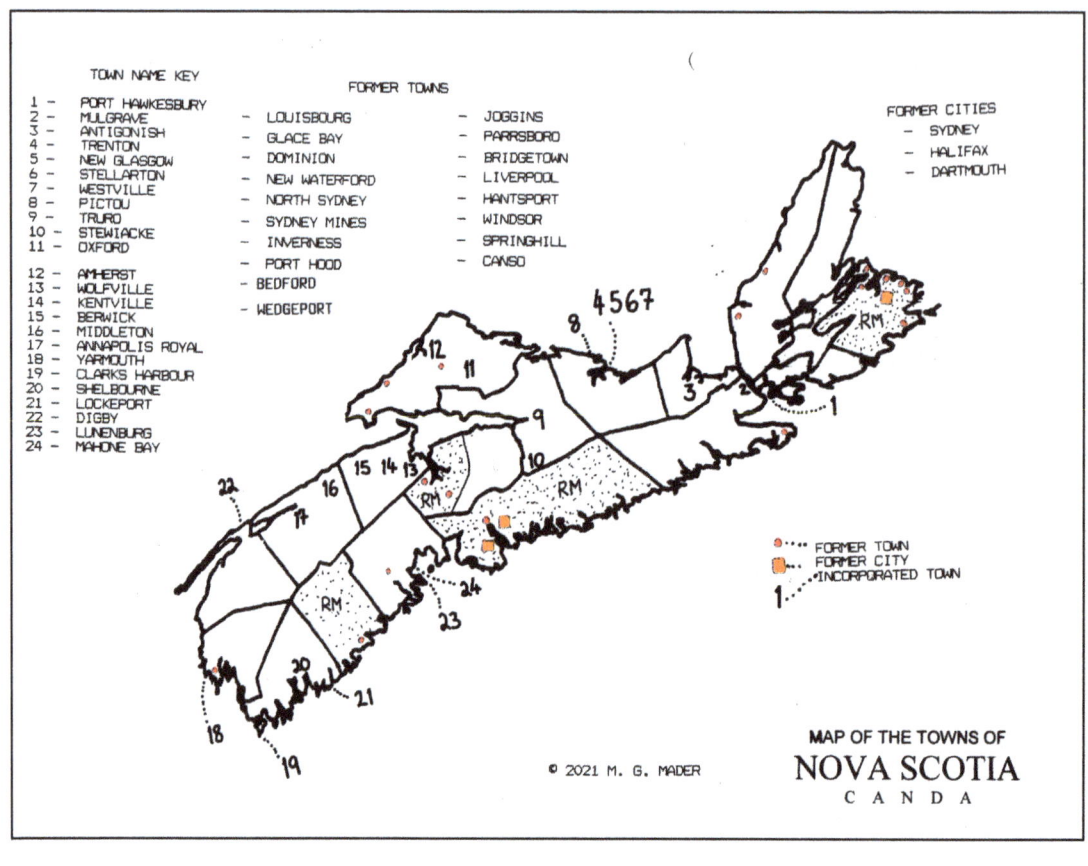

Map of the current and former incorporated towns and cities of Nova Scotia. Nova Scotia has not had any incorporated cities since the amalgamation of the cities of Dartmouth and Halifax into the Halifax Regional Municipality in 1996.

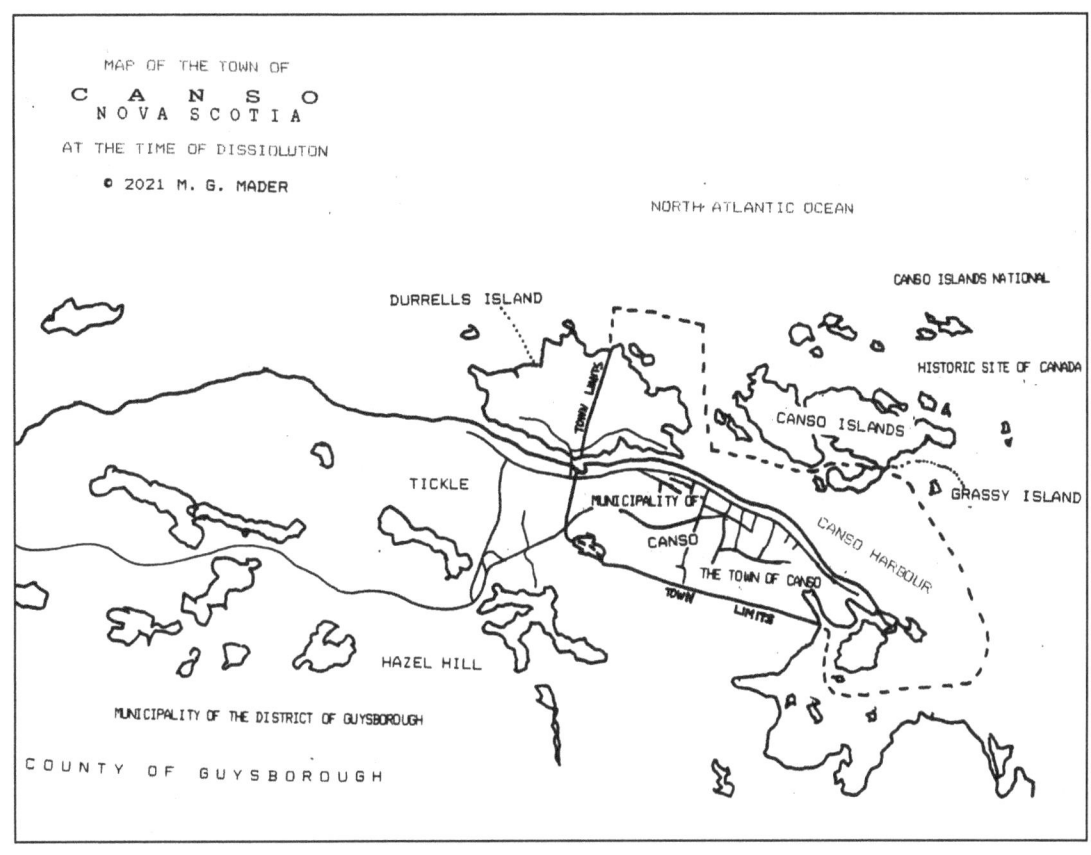

Map of the former Town of Canso and surrounding communities. The former town of Canso municipality took in the entire community of Canso as well as several outlying islands, including Grassy Island, as shown on the map to the right. Interestingly, the town also took in approximately one half of Durells Island, although the bridge connecting the island to the mainland was outside of the town limits. The bridge to Durells Island collapsed in 2020, with the dramatic incident being caught on video and posted to the World Wide Web.

AFTERWORD

This book is not, nor was it ever envisioned to be, a history of Canso. There are other books that provide a detailed history of the town. Rather, this book is a snapshot of Canso as it was in June 2012, as the town was winding up operations and preparing to be taken over by the Municipality of the District of Guysborough. The inspiration for the book came to me when I was working at the *Caper Times* campus newspaper at Cape Breton University. I had written a series of articles called 'A sign of the times' about the approaching dissolution of the Town of Canso. During my discussions with then-mayor of Canso Frank Fraser, and after coming across a commemorative booklet prepared by the Municipality of the County of Cape Breton at the McConnell Memorial Library in Sydney, the idea for a commemorative booklet for Canso slowly formed within my mind.

The first hurdle that I faced was finding a way to fund the printing of several hundred copies of the booklet that I hoped to write. It was May 2012 and I had just finished my first year at university. I had been hired as the editor-in-chief of the Students' Union-owned campus newspaper, where I had previously been employed as an advertising salesperson. I decided that I would try to get local businesses to sponsor the booklet in exchange for including their name and logo in the booklet and on a companion website I was developing. I thought that perhaps I could use my position at the campus newspaper to facilitate the project, primarily by providing name recognition when I sought sponsorship from businesses. My dear friend Mary Suzanne had at the same time been successful in becoming one of the Students' Union vice-presidents. Mary Suzanne and the other Students' Union executive officers put their faith in me when I presented them with my proposal to prepare and publish a sponsored booklet commemorating the Town of Canso. Thus, the Canso Booklet Committee was formed. It was a strange idea but I reasoned it would help promote the newspaper and the Students' Union by showing we were active in the community.

Having permission to proceed, I then began to seek sponsorship. Then-Cape Breton Canso MP Rodger Cuzner agreed to sponsor the publication and I am eternally grateful to him for this. Likewise, the Municipality of the District of Guysborough agreed, with the assistance of then-Warden Lloyd Hines. The Canso branch of the Bank of Montreal also purchased a sponsorship package, as did the Cape Breton University Students' Union.

Enough funds had been raised to proceed with the booklet and I arranged to visit Canso on a Saturday. It was a great visit and I spent a few hours with Frank Fraser, the last mayor of Canso. We met at the Town Office and I explained my proposed publication and he enthusiastically supported my endeavour. He gave me a tour of the historic building, after which we returned to his office. He showed me the Town's copy of the prolific 2004 book on the history of Canso and Mr Fraser allowed me to borrow it as a resource when writing my book, after making me promise to bring it back (which, of course, I had always intended to do). It was a thick tome and was much prised by Mr Fraser and the other townspeople. It would prove an enormous help to me as I embarked on writing a small book about a town I had only visited once.

Unfortunately, the time had passed quickly and I now had only a fortnight to research, write, design, and print the booklet. Two hundred copies of the original edition were printed. As the editor position at the newspaper only paid during the school year, I was working full time throughout the week at an unrelated summer job. My nights were spent at the newspaper offices at Cape Breton University and my freshly hired staff assisted me in administrative tasks for the book. Finally, the deadline to get the book to the printer approach and I ended up working on the design until late into the night. Exhausted, I finally clicked send on the email to the print shop containing the PDF of the finished booklet. I then drove home, slept for a few hours, and went to my day job the next morning. I wish this was the end of the story, but frustratingly, it isn't.

It was during my lunch break later that day that a thought occurred to me: I had exported the booklet several times whilst proof reading before sending the file to the printer; had I exported the final, proof read and corrected version to PDF before sending it in? It being 2012, I attempted to log into my email on my not-so-smart mobile phone, but had no luck. I rang the printer, knowing the last thing I had added was a link to the companion website on the first page. I asked if a website address appeared above the author name on the first page and was told no address was present. I had sent the wrong file! I asked the printer if they could hold off on printing the booklet and they said they would. I explained a new file would be sent as soon as I could that day and that the correct file for printing was the file with a webpage address on the first page above the author name. After work, I drove straight to the office, logged onto my computer, and sent the correct file. I spoke with the printer again the next day to confirm which file needed to be printed and which could be deleted. I was relieved, but had a nagging feeling that something would go wrong.

Imagine my horror on Friday, the day before the Town Closing Ceremony, to find – after all of that ringing and emailing – that the printer had printed the wrong file. I rang the printer immediately, who said they could reprint the booklets but it would take until Monday. This just would not work, I needed the booklets by 7am the next day so that I could drive them to the Canso fire brigade building, where the Town Closing Ceremony was being held.

Embarrassed by the errors in the booklet, I drove to Canso the following morning with the box of booklets in my passenger seat. I handed a copy to every person who attended, explaining to each person that the printer had made an error and there were likely to be typos inside but that the correct version could be read as an eBook online.

When I finally sat down, it turned out that I was near Marney Simmons, then-mayor of the nearby Town of Mulgrave. She was very impressed with the booklet, despite the printer error, and asked if she could take the extra booklets with her to display and hand out in the Mulgrave Museum, which her town operated in the summer months. I agreed and had hoped to visit the museum to see my booklet, but sadly never had the opportunity to do so.

The next time that I visited Canso was with my aunt Barb and cousin Sara. The Town of Canso no longer existed and the welcome sign at the town limits had been replaced with a Municipality of the District of Guysborough-branded sign. Although I had written about the town, I had never had the opportunity to visit it as a tourist and we enjoyed a few leisurely hours sightseeing, including visiting the Whitman House Museum, the highlight of which was the widow's walk on the roof.

I remained editor of the *Caper Times* for two years after the original publication, and became vice-president of the Students' Union in 2014. In 2013, I bought a disused offset printing press from a secondary school in Cole Harbour, Nova Scotia as part of a plan to start my own publishing company. I did eventually start my own company in 2017, after emigrating to Australia where I now live, though I've found that outsourcing the printing of books is much more economical than printing your own publications. Since I first published the original booklet, I have always wanted to revisit what I call my 'Canso book' but it took me eight years to do so. In 2019, I published a facsimile of the original edition as an online eBook. I then began preparing an updated revised edition, which has become this tenth anniversary edition in reference to the 10-year anniversary of the dissolution of the Town of Canso in June 2022. Initially, I had reservations about the limited written content of this book, though with time these concerns have faded as more of the public buildings in Canso have been demolished and the value of my extensive collection of pre-dissolution photographs becomes clearer. Ten years on, I believe it captures Canso at the end of its time as an incorporated town very well.

                     M. G. MADER
                Melbourne · November 2021

The emblem of the Canso Booklet Committee, which published the original edition of this publication.

ACKNOWLEGMENTS

The original edition of this publication would not have been possible without the generous support of the Cape Breton University Students' Union, Mr Rodger Cuzner (former parliamentarian representing Cape Breton-Canso in the Canadian Parliament), the Municipality of the District of Guysborough, and the Canso Branch of the Bank of Montreal.

Thank you also to Ms Mary Suzanne MacEachern, Publisher and Chairperson of the *Caper Times* 2012-2013, as well the 2012-2013 staff of the *Caper Times* for their support of this project.

Finally, His Worship Frank Fraser, the last mayor of the former Town of Canso, provided moral and contextual support to this project for which I am forever grateful.

THE MAYORS OF CANSO
1901 - 2012

E. C. Whitman	1901-1911
H. A. Rice	1911-1924
H. F. Robinson	1924-1925
J. A. Ferguson	1926-1931; 1938-1942
D. J. McNeary	1932-1933
L. R. Croucher	1934-1937
Cecil O. Boyd	1942-1943 (Acting); 1943-1946
R. E. Jamieson	1946-1952
Kenneth Lumsden	1952-1954
W. A. Pembroke	1954-1956
Walter NcNeary	1956-1961
Jim Hanlon	1962-1965; 1968-1973
Dr H. J. Bland	1966-1967
Jerome Lumsden	1973-1977
Barry Lumsden	1977-1979
Raymond White	1979-1993
Frank Fraser	1993-1994; 2000-2012 (Dissolution)
Ronald George	1994-2000

ABOUT THE AUTHOR

M. G. MADER is a town and country planner working in local government within the Victorian planning system. He has a Master of Planning and Environment from the Royal Melbourne Institute of Technology and a Bachelor of Arts with a focus on Political Science from Cape Breton University. He has a strong interest in local government, democratic community governance, and local history. He lives with his partner in Melbourne, Australia.

www.ingramcontent.com/pod-product-compliance
Lightning Source LLC
Chambersburg PA
CBHW061145010526
44118CB00026B/2880